PERSUASIVE PARABLES

W. Reid Claypoole

Order this book online at www.trafford.com
or email orders@trafford.com

Most Trafford titles are also available at major online book retailers.

Printed in the United States of America.

ISBN: 978-1-4269-4078-1 (sc)
ISBN: 978-1-4269-4080-4 (e)

Library of Congress Control Number: 2010913057

*Our mission is to efficiently provide the world's finest, most comprehensive book publishing service,
enabling every author to experience success. To find out how to publish your book, your way, and have it
available worldwide, visit us online at www.trafford.com*

Trafford rev. 09/08/2010

 www.trafford.com

North America & international
toll-free: 1 888 232 4444 (USA & Canada)
phone: 250 383 6864 ♦ fax: 812 355 4082

This book is dedicated to the memory of
Annie Elizabeth (Bowser) Claypoole
Granma C.
1878-1967

She was the mother of 6 boys and 4 girls.
She was the grandmother of 19
and an inspiration to all who knew her.

PERSUASIVE PARABLES

Parables are stories told to illustrate a point, usually moral or spiritual. The author chose this format to communicate the lessons of life, learned the hard way. Circumstances always appear more clearly as one looks back in retrospect. Perhaps young readers will be creative and not repeat the ill-considered mistakes that I've made.

Forty+ years of interviewing, hiring and training sales/marketing people convinced me that they needed ego boosting. Also as I worked with college juniors and seniors, only a select few aspired to starting their career as a salesperson. Almost to an individual, they saw selling as a low esteem profession. They had developed little regard for the salespeople they encountered on a day-to-day basis. The few exceptions, to this generality, had a mother or father who had been successful in sales. Certainly I have encountered the con-type, hustler or misdirected person who carried the moniker of salesman. So, the conundrum continues: "Why am I so proud to call myself a salesman?"

In the process of answering this question to my own satisfaction, I considered the concept of "low pressure vs high pressure". Based on decades of working with salespeople, I came to believe that there is no such thing as "low pressure/high pressure". Actually the process of selling involves the exertion of pressure. If pressure is lacking, you are a high paid visitor, not a salesperson. The difference has nothing to do with pressure but has everything to do with the attitude and skill with which a decision is sought. The key attitude is based on the premise that

"I am here to use my knowledge and experience to help you make a decision that is in your best interest". Many times, I was complimented by having a client say, "Bill, I like doing business with you because you don't try to pressure me into buying." The reality was that they perceived that I had their best interest at heart and they trusted me. The pressure was there, it just wasn't felt. Why?

The answer to this question resides in my definition of salesmanship: ***Salesmanship is the effective use of all of your previous knowledge and experience to help someone make a decision*** which is in their best interest.

The focus should not be on making a sale. Rather, it should be on helping a client make a good decision. When they can trust you to do that, you are always welcome in their home or place of business. You can walk tall and be proud.

WALK IN MY MOCASSINS

Indians have a saying, "in order to understand someone else, you need to walk in their moccasins for two moons". Since many of the ideas that I am going to share with you are personal and private, you should find the walk interesting and stimulating. Perhaps, after that, you will relate and make the generational transition better as you hear my persuasive parables. As you peruse and browse through these pages, Granma Claypoole should be as real to you as her memories are to me. I plan to salt the book with the homilies that she used on a daily basis to explain the actions and attitudes of other people. I hope they imbed these thoughts on your memory bank and make them useful to you in coping with the daily dilemmas of life and the vagaries of communicating with others.

My walk began on a dairy farm in western Pennsylvania owned by my paternal grandparents. On this 135 acre tract, they parented 10 children, 6 boys and 4 girls. They were all 5' 10" or taller. Granma was 5'4". But there was never any doubt about who was in charge. She ruled in the old fashioned way: Absolutely. Further, I was one of the 19 grandchildren this union produced. To a farm family, more children meant more workers who only had to be housed, fed and clothed; not paid. Only four of the grandchildren earned a college degree and Granma was suspicious of the work ethic of those who did. In fact, about ten years out of college, I returned for a family 4th of July. Granma knew that I was in the "drug" business. (Johnson & Johnson). She confided to family members later that she was worried about young Bill. "He looks prosperous but his hands are not calloused. Is he into something dishonest"?

Being raised on a dairy farm creates a very special attitude toward work. The memories of getting out of bed into a house with no central heating at 4am; rounding up the cows in the dark; feeding, milking and cleaning up after the cows are etched in my mind. This may explain why I have so little patience with the thirty somethings who complain of "burn-out". Burn-out is not a concept understood by dairy farmers. Milking cows is a twice-a-day, 7 days a week and 365 days a year job. Vacations are largely unknown to dairy farmers because no one else wants to milk your cows unless you are desperately ill or have suffered a natural disaster. When I hear someone say that they are "burned-out", to me they are really saying, "I'm too damn lazy to do what it takes to succeed".

The best job security comes from

being worth more than you are paid.

Granma C

Some of the good memories of life on the farm were the wonderful breakfasts that we were served at 7 am when we got in from the barn. And the smell of wind-dried bedsheets that we slipped between after a hard days work. Also the clean sensation of the Saturday night bath. There was a sense of accomplishment in mastering new tasks; seeing a beautifully plowed field with its straight furrows and picking fresh peaches or tomatoes that you had planted, hoed, pruned and tended.

Many times, particularly in the Spring, I would watch my father and most of my relatives kneel in a freshly cultivated field and run the soil through their fingers. It seemed to connected them to their souls. I tried it, but I didn't get that feeling. Not having much of a lust for dairy farming, I had to explain to my father one day that I wanted to take a job in town at 15 cents/hour. I had to walk or push my scooter the three miles into town and back. It still beat the 50 cents per day that Dad paid me to work from dawn to post-dark. He doubted my determination and told me that my old job would be waiting for me anytime I wanted it back. I never really worked on the farm after that except to help out in a pinch or at harvest time. Milking cows that switched me with their tail or stepped into an almost full bucket of milk were to be a thing of the past.

In a few short years, my moccasins enrolled at the University of Pittsburgh in Pre-Med. Since college degrees were not a part of our family culture, it was understood, by all concerned, that I was on my own. Dad didn't want to waste hard earned money on a kid who was too lazy to work on the farm. Fortunately, I won a $ 1000/semester scholarship (1950) which covered tuition and books. I paid my room rent from money made selling sterling silver door-to-door and I was given three meals a day for bussing dishes in the college cafeteria.

In the summers, I organized a crew of Pitt boys. We painted houses, nightclubs, and the bridges of Armstrong County PA (not Madison County). At no time did I feel sorry for myself. In fact, I believe that working my way through college taught me the realities of communicating and working effectively with other people. I certainly never developed the luxury of looking down on people who worked hard (blue-collar)for a living.

However, although I got my degree in Pre-Med, I was not accepted into medical school largely because I could not show available money to assure the school that I had the resources needed to complete medical training. If they started a class of 96 students, they wanted to graduate 96 doctors. In those days school loans were not available. Thus began my career as a medical detailman for J&J. Parables to follow will fill you in on the trail left by my moccasins. I have tried to give you a mental picture of where this ambitious Yankee kid was coming from and why anything else I did in life seemed like play compared with cow's teats on a cold morning.

If you want to predict what someone

is going to do in the future, just look and

see what they did in the past.

Granma C.

ARE PERSUASIVE COMMUNICATORS MADE OR BORN?

The answer is YES. Certainly everyone is not meant to make a living as a salesperson but we all must polish our persuasive skills to get through this world more easily and productively. As you know, there are born extroverts who are self motivated and they are blessed with naturally good communication skills. However, I have seen shy, introverted people with speech impediments or crippling injuries be successful as salespeople. I particularly remember a medical detail man who stuttered. He worked for Wyeth Pharmaceuticals. One of their products was Wyanoid rectal suppositories. As he left the doctor's office he would give the doctor some samples of Wyanoids and say, "Doctor, if-f- you can-n-n-t fi-fi find anyth-th-thing else to do with th-th-these, stick th-th-them up your ass". You guessed it. He sold more Wyanoids than any other three salesmen in the country.

Johnson & Johnson hired me fresh out of school and sent me to the dynamic Dixie division. The Dixie division was the top sales division in the country. My territory was to be central Georgia based out of Macon (yes, the same territory that Sherman covered on his March to the Sea).

My District Sales Mgr, DuPont Murphey was a bourbon drinking, dyed-in-grey-wool Southerner. His secretary Nancy Pless-had a Georgia accent that could melt the fuzz off a peach. I was a wet-behind-the-ears Yankee who had been foisted upon him by those folks in Noo Jersay. Dupont's words of greeting to me were: "If a Yankee can sell in central Georgia, he can sell anywhere in the world". How's that for southern hospitality?

At our first district sales meeting, "I was Yankee fresh meat". I was totally intimidated and couldn't stop my father's words from ringing in my ears; "I never raised a son of mine to be a (sic) salesman". As I listened to these garrulous veterans regale each other with their exploits, I could hardly keep my mouth from hanging open and my jaw off the floor. I looked around the room to see what these successful salespeople had in common. One was short and another was tall; one was thin and another was fat; one was unkempt and another was well groomed; one had a polished vocabulary and another sounded like a truck driver on his CB; one was old and another was young. There was no visible composite that I could use for a pattern.

It was some twenty years later that I learned about the two characteristics that successful salespeople have in common: 1) a high ego need to persuade and 2) high empathy. Successful persuaders have both of these characteristics to a high degree. I learned this from an industrial psychologist in New York City. Dr. Sid tested all of our screened applicants. He made me a deal that if he recommended someone, they would be among our top sales producers within a year or he would find me another candidate at no charge. His record was incredible. He never missed. As I was leaving the Company to take a bigger job in Tennessee, I asked him for his secret. That is when he told me about Ego-Need-to-Persuade and Empathy. Let's talk further about these two characteristics which are hard to find at a high level in the same individual High-ego-need-to-persuade, without a high level of empathy, creates the stereotypical salesperson; the one who leaves tire treads up the chest of the buyer. The major problem with this type is that the only thing that works is their sending set. Their listening set is inoperable. They are intent on "making a sale". They believe that you <u>talk</u> people into buying. They run roughshod over cues and hints sent out by the buyer. Thus they are unable to project themselves into the position of the buyer. Unfortunately, sales work attracts a lot of this personality type and they have created a bad image for salespeople in general. Their high motivation and energy are valuable assets but a manager of this type has to constantly remind them to "practice delayed response and listen". However, in my experience, you cannot teach someone to be empathetic. The radar screen of a High-Ego-Need-To-Persuade just does not pick up signals.

For example, Tom worked as an account executive for me. Many times I would tell him to listen to what the client is saying. His answer was, "I know what he is saying and I don't care". Believe it or not, he not only had problems with customers, he had problems in his personal relationships and with fellow employees. The skills that I am talking about are important if you want to become an effective communicator and want to have the capability to motivate and manage others.

> *If you think you can or you*
>
> *think you can't, you are right.*
>
> *Granma C.*

I was a field sales manager when ***Empathy*** was discovered. For years thereafter, those who hired sales people thought they had discovered the Open Sesame (remember this was the magic word that the genie taught to Aladdin) to hiring effective sales people. Finally, we realized that these sympathetic, sensitive empathizers were so good at placing themselves into the feelings of the buyer that the buyer was having more effect on them than they were having on the buyer. Instead of coming back with an order, they returned and recited in total detail the problems of their buyers and pleaded with the company to make changes and accommodations on a custom basis to satisfy the whims of the client.

My example of an empathizer was Dick. He was a nine year veteran of the FBI who wanted to get into sales. He was hired because of his obvious people skills. He could walk through an office and tell you who was having personal problems that morning. His difficulty in sales was that he became a reservoir for other people's problems and hardly ever closed a sale. Dick was a strong, customer-oriented sales person but he should have gone into social work. He was helping people make decisions that had nothing to do with what he was being paid to do.

Occasionally you find a person with both a 1) high ego need to persuade and a 2) high level of empathy. That individual cannot miss in persuasive skills. There are tests to measure these characteristics and a good psychologist can administer them for you. Interestingly enough, after I became aware of this fact, I knew what I was looking for and did a better job of identifying them myself. Further, you can now look at yourself and answer honestly, "Do I possess these characteristics?"

> *There are only two kinds*
>
> *of salespeople; those who produce*
>
> *orders and those who produce excuses.*
>
> *Granma C.*

A CULTURE SHOCK

The best direction to ride a horse is in the direction it is going and my horse was headed south. I remember calling my wife and telling her that I had been assigned from the training school in New Jersey to the Macon, GA territory. She said, "Where"? I said, "You know, Makin". After a 1,200 mile drive straight south, my pregnant wife and I arrived in Macon and parked in front of Ingleside Drugstore on Sunday afternoon. I got out of our black, 2-door, 1950 Plymouth coupe to get a city map. As I walked back to the car, I noticed a young boy kicking my Pennsylvania license plates. "The War between the States" was still being fought in Macon, GA. These people in central Georgia *had been raised to hate Yankees.* The words of my district sales manager came back to me, "If a Yankee can sell in central Georgia, he can sell anywhere in the world".

On one of my first sales trips to Milledgeville, GA (this was one of the cities destroyed by Sherman), I noticed that the stores downtown were all closed. So I asked a man nearby, "What's going on today"? He withered me with a hateful stare and informed me that "Today is January 19, the birthday of Robert E Lee". On another trip to Fitzgerald, GA. I introduced myself to the pharmacist/owner. He slowly looked me up and down and asked, "Where are you from"? "I'm from Macon". "No" he said, "I mean before that". Do you get the picture? Proving that a Yankee could sell in central Georgia was going to be a challenge.

Johnson & Johnson devised an insidious motivational tool. It was called the Monthly Rating Report. As a salesperson you were rated monthly with 122 other U.S. salespeople. We were rated on *dollar volume increase over the previous year's sales in seven product catergories.* The average of your monthly standings determined your monthly position and it was cumulative. It was well known that the bottom 10% had a habit of disappearing. It was also well known that the top 10% got nice bonuses and promotions. Although my young family's discretionary funds were very limited, I rented a post office box so that I could get this report a day or two early. I also discovered that my territory was a new territory made up of the scraps that other Dixiecrats didn't want. I reported to Macon in June and by December was in the middle of the Rating Report. For the next six years, I made the TOP TEN every year. (Not bad for a Yankee).

Grow where you are planted.

Granma C.

How did I do it? I didn't know, so I asked Dr. Ed. Brannen, a Macon gynecologist, who prescribed everything we made, "What am I doing right"? His answer was very revealing. He said, "You've studied my patients in the waiting room and know the problems that I'm facing. You have prepared yourself before coming into my office. You tell me what your product will do for my patients and you make sure that it is stocked at the local pharmacies. "You don't waste my time". Although he was a native Georgian he wanted to do business with someone who could help him solve problems, deliver better care to his patients and make money. This formula will work for you selling anything, anywhere in the world.

After three years in Macon, I turned in my resignation to take a position with New York Life Ins. Instead, J&J promoted me to the Kansas City territory with a hefty pay raise and a title. In addition to learning my way around a major city, I had the good fortune to take the Dale Carnegie course. Now I realize that this doesn't sound like a big deal, but it was a life changer for me. Dale Carnegie Public Speaking Course was really a course to build self-confidence and improve one's human relation skills. I learned basic concepts such as "Give another person a good reputation to live up to", Praise works like sugar, criticism works like salt and Be prepared, Be brief and Be seated".

As you heard earlier, I was raised in an environment where you got little praise for doing a good job. The minimum expectation was a good job. The only recognition my father gave me was when I screwed up. Naturally, I carried this same critical attitude into my personal relationships, including marriage. Oh how, our relationship improved when I began practicing my Dale Carnegie lessons at home. My wife and children were pleasantly surprised at my recognition of their special efforts to please me. A goodly part of sales skills is the practice of being considerate, communicative and appreciative.

Keep your words soft and sweet.

You never know when you will have to eat them.

Granma C.

Job changes and promotions gave my family the opportunity to adjust to living in Macon, GA; Kansas City, MO, Cuyahoga Falls and Cincinnati, OH: Darien, CT; Greenville, TN; Odessa and Dallas, TX. My sales territories spanned all of the U.S.A. east of the Rockies. Finally, as Director of Marketing, I covered the 48 states (Yes, it was before Alaska and Hawaii). The major value of this moving and adjusting taught me the importance of setting your watch to local time. By that I mean that people, where you move, don't want you to tell them what is wrong with where they live. Nor do they want to listen to you complain about how much better things were where you came from.

I loved a bumper sticker that appeared in Texas during the mid-80's. There was a job boom in Texas that attracted people from all over the country. The sticker said, "If you don't like Texas, take Interstate 30 East". People who live and love where they live, don't take kindly to criticism from people just passing through. Anywhere I have lived has been a combination of advantages and disadvantages. If you focus on the disadvantages, you are unhappy. If you focus on the advantages, you are happy. The greatest freedom that each of us has is the freedom to choose our own attitude.

If you didn't like where you came from,

you probably won't like it here.

Granma C.

WHAT DO GOOD SALESPEOPLE HAVE IN COMMON?

Only about 20% of the people who make a living selling are GOOD salespeople. But that is equally true of most other professions. Since you are reading this to help yourself to become a better communicator, let's discuss what GOOD communicators have in common. In my experience, I have found that people who succeed in sales have six common characteristics:

1.   Self management discipline

2.   Initiative

3.   Problem solving attitude

4.   Patience and persistence

5.   Good social skills

6.   Good personal hygiene and appearance

Self Management is easy to talk about and most everyone believes that they are good at this. However, this is probably the number one cause of failure. People who lack this skill will always have an excuse for not getting things done or for jobs not having a successful outcome. If you can't manage yourself, what makes you think that you can manage anyone else?

Self Management starts with discipline and time management. A boss of mine drilled into my head, "If you aren't ten minutes early, you are late". I've noticed when I leave early for an appointment, all the lights are green and I don't have any flat tires. Even if things run against me, I have time to make a phone call or take corrective action. The net result is that you earn a *reputation* for being prompt. My reputation for being punctual is so good that when I screw up, business associates and friends fear that something serious has happened to me. I just believe that being prompt and keeping your appointments is a matter of good manners and consideration for others. Always remember that you have probably earned and deserve whatever reputation you have. A bad reputation is almost impossible to erase or replace.

If you point your finger at someone else,

three fingers are pointing back at you.

Granma C.

The basic planning device for salespeople is an itinerary. I've worked with enough men and women to know that most of them fight doing an itinerary. The explanation usually is, "I never know when a customer is going to call and take me completely off my itinerary" or "Do you want me to make sales calls or fill out itinerary forms?" Certainly customers call you when they have problems and for the most part they are real. A good service attitude would cause you to drop what you are doing and head straight across your territory (yes, these calls usually come from the other side of your territory). Still, I would like to tell you a true story.

At one time in my career, I was selling plastic raw resin in Michigan, Ohio, Kentucky and western Pennsylvania--a big territory. I believed in and routinely took the time to create a 3-week itinerary. The process of putting together my itinerary forced me to organize my travel time and prioritize my sales calls according to potential. Due directly to the organization of my time, I covered this huge territory, increased our market share and drove the company car approximately 30,000 miles/year. This relatively low mileage was due to the fact that when a customer called in a panic, I was able to tell him that I was planning to be at his plant next Tuesday. At least 2 out of 3 times the customer would say, "OK Bill, it can wait until then". Just imagine how much time this enabled me to put to more productive use than driving my car all over the territory. You don't make sales driving all night.

The real clincher in the above story is that when I was promoted to our NYC office, the man who followed me into the territory wouldn't do itineraries. During his first year, he was driving 45,000 miles/year and our share of market was dropping. He was terminated, not for being unwilling to work hard but for not being productive. Several years later this same man was in town and invited me to lunch. Vince was now National Sales Manager for a chemical company in Houston. At lunch he thanked me for the lesson learned and told me that he is now the most demanding of managers when it comes to expecting his people to do itineraries.

Plan your sales routing by taking into account the work habits of your customers, the sales potential of different clients and the best use of your non-selling time. Be a self starter and be able to work unsupervised. Show respect for your own time and others will do so also.

People don't plan to fail. They fail to plan.

Granma C.

Initiative is defined as taking the steps that lead to action. Leaders are people who show initiative. They make things happen. Successful people don't sit around waiting for things to happen. In fact, one of the oldest sale's axioms is, "Nothing happens until someone sells something". You need to be in an action mode. My business partner used to say, "Bill is in a fail- forward mode". I took this as a compliment. BE IN CHARGE OF CHANGE. People who thought of themselves as being in the buggy-whip business would not have gone out of business if they had thought of themselves as being in the transportation business.

Individuals who display initiative used to be called self starters. They are people who empower themselves. They also run the risk of making a mistake or being wrong. That isn't bad. However, you do need to be creative in making mistakes, i.e. don't make the same mistake twice. For heaven's sake, learn from your mistakes and grow. Truthfully, you learn more from your mistakes than you do from your successes.

Experience is the thing you get when you

are doing something that you shouldn't be doing.

Granma C.

A lot of people kick around the term, "professional". What do you think that means? To me, it means that no matter how big your reputation is, every time you run out on the field, you have to earn your reputation all over again. Never say, "I've paid my dues". You're only as good as your last job.

It is important for you to realize whether you are a creative or a maintenance sales person. Both are necessary and valuable. But the more creative one is used by companies to go in and clean up a territory that is in bad shape. This type is hard working, assertive and can be abrasive. Thus the creative type of salesperson is moved from one territory to another at 3-5 years intervals. The maintenance salesperson gets along well with people and frequently may work the same territory from 20 years to life. Maintenance types have a lot of staying power and are the backbone of any sales force.

The professional sales person has to learn to deal with rejection. You have to learn to not take it personal and to not let rejection interfere with follow-up calls on prospects or customers. The salesperson with initiative will use whatever is learned from the rejection to help him/her succeed on the next call. Job security comes from doing more than is expected of you.

When the customer says "NO"

is when the selling process begins.

Granma C.

A Problem Solving Attitude involves imagination and creativity. It is a cultivated attitude that is constantly looking for a better way to do things or to make good things happen. When you dedicate yourself to becoming a problem solver instead of just a problem finder, you will be worth more to yourself and to your employer. It involves looking at things from a different perspective. I use words such as minify, magnify and modify to help me look at things differently. It helps to imagine yourself as the problem. It also helps to think of wild and crazy ideas, then sleep on them.

Your subconscious is a powerful ally. Put it to work for you. Define the problem you want solved, in its simplest form, and then sleep on it. This lets your brain scan all of your stored data. You may wake up in the middle of the night and say, "Aha, that's it". If you do, you had better write it down on that tablet beside your bed or you'll most likely forget it by morning. Some quiet time or reverie with nature will frequently serve the same purpose as sleeping on it. It is vitally important that you have defined the problem in it simplest form. The following is a real life example:

My family and I were members of a small church in Prairie Village, KS. The church was badly in need of painting and we didn't have enough money. But was that our problem stated in its simplest form? No. That problem statement left us with the choices of abandoning the building, finding a way to raise the money or finding some other creative way to solve the problem. We finally stated our problem as, "How can we get the men and women of the church to give several hours of their time to help paint the church?" Once we stated our problem thusly, we were on our way to solving it. The church was painted. Everyone was proud of their contribution.

Unfortunately, we Americans have a national characteristic of starting to work on solutions before we have adequately defined the problem. We are a Ready, Fire, Aim society. We seldom have time to do it right the first time but we always have time to do it over.

A problem well defined is already half solved.

Granma C.

Also, problem-solving-behavior can be a unique form of creativity. But be sure to differentiate between originality and creativity. Originality is doing something that has never been done before. Creativity is recombining or putting things together differently than has been done before to solve a new problem. Creativity is based on use of prior experience. That is why older people are actually more creative that younger people. They have a deeper well of experience to draw upon. Be in the idea business. Ideas are always welcome.

12% of the people in this world think.

12 % think they think and the other 76% are

sitting around waiting for someone to write a slogan.

Granma C.

The 1st Law of Creativity says, "When everyone is doing the same thing, it is time to do something different". We see taken-for-granted ideas around us every day e.g. wheelchairs (both chairs and wheels were invented long before someone solved a problem by putting them together). Or someone said, "I'd like to go to sleep and wake up to music". Both the alarm clock and radio were invented long before they were put together. What about the paint roller? Who was the person who came up with the idea of rolling on paint after generations of putting on paint with a brush? Practice looking for unconventional ways to do things. Develop a problem solving attitude. A good place to start is with recurring problems. Creativity comes from a questioning, problem-solving attitude.

Problems are unsolved opportunities.

Granma C.

Persistence and Patience are <u>not</u> generally thought of in connection with each other. But I especially like to link them because I believe that persistence is patience in action. Patience is looked upon as being complacent and willing to wait for whatever is going to happen. Rather, I believe that patience is a strong characteristic because it embodies the idea that you have to allow time for things to happen. Persistence has a time tenacity that is a major factor in the success of some salespeople and the failure of others. Most sales are not made as the result of a dazzling presentation. Instead, the sale happens because of the follow-up and follow-through which is a combination of persistence and patience. The following is an example:

Our agency had the opportunity to make a new business pitch for the Kaepa tennis shoe account. However, we were not selected. The account went to an agency in Chicago. In spite of the loss, I continued to read all of the trade and consumer magazines. When I saw an article that pertained to the marketing or manufacturing of tennis shoes, I would clip it and send it along to Tom, the president of Kaepa. After about 18 months, I got a call and it was Tom. He said, "We'd like for you to come to San Antonio this week". Naturally, I agreed to be there at their convenience. However, I did ask, "Tom, do you mind telling what I should be prepared to discuss"? He said, "We want to give you our account". Have you already guessed why we got the account? "You showed more interest in our business, not being our agency, than our agency showed".

Success comes from doing the things that

people who fail are unwilling to do.

Granma C.

Vince Lombardi of the Green Bay Packers evidenced persistence and patience in his now famous statement, "We never lost a football game. Occasionally we ran out of time". He did not believe in giving up when it came to attaining his lofty goals. He wouldn't keep a player on his team who did not exemplify this same attitude. This is why he was one of the winningest coaches in professional football. Another winner was Leo Durocher, coach of the Brooklyn Dodgers who said, "Good losers get too used to losing". Both of these successful motivators knew the importance of persistence.

If it is to be, it is up to me.

Granma C.

Please understand the importance of patience and persistence. The combination will make you or your firm "unforgettable". Becoming unforgettable is not result of a great presentation although this is a good way to start. (Reread the Kaepa story above). Becoming unforgettable comes from innovative ways to remind your prospect, your boss or your banker, of the benefits that come from placing their trust in you. Call regularly in person. Stay in contact by phone. Find reasons to communicate with them in writing between other contacts. Take the time to learn about their problems and concerns. This tells the other person that you are thinking about his/her concerns when you are separated, not just when you pull up in front of his door. You become "unforgettable". When they need your product or services, they will call you first. It is the objective of all persuasive communications. You should be striving to become Top-Of-Mind.

Good Social Skills are based on being considerate of others. There are appropriate and inappropriate things to do and say. You certainly have the right to violate any of such guidelines. However, it is important that you know what the rules are and know that if you violate them, you are consciously going against the best advice on how to conduct yourself in public and individually with other people. Lettica Baldridge writes one of the best and most up-to-date books for business people called, "Complete Guide To Executive Manners". Even if you aren't an executive yet, knowing the right things to do will greatly accelerate your advancement. Perhaps a few of my most embarrassing moments may serve to make this point.

> *Saying I don't know is a sign of*
>
> *strength, not a sign of weakness.*
>
> *Granma C.*

I can look back now with amusement on my own rocky road to some degree of sophistication. On the way, I made a lot of faux pas and tell them only that you may realize how much shorter your journey needs to be than mine.

You will learn that becoming a sophisticated person is a lifelong, learning experience. For example, the first time I was confronted with someone wanting me to order red snapper, I declined this delicacy because I didn't know what it was. And with a name like red snapper, I could only imagine the eating complexities of a lobster. It was later in life that I learned to love red snapper and to enjoy getting out every tender morsel of a lobster.

On another occasion, I was speaking on the Rh factor to a medical group and was the guest of Dr. Helen Reed Deal. She wanted me to order me a filet mignon. I had visions of something that had little doilies on its legs. I begged off by telling her that I preferred hamburger steak. I'll bet she chuckled for years over that episode. Further, I had been trained to think of the starving little children in China and I should eat everything on my plate. Thus, later in life I felt that cleaning your plate also meant eating the lettuce your shrimp cocktail sat on. If someone else had not ordered my first shrimp cocktail, I would probably have rejected it also because it sounded like some strange drink. How much smarter I would have been to admit that I didn't know and ask questions. <u>Bluffing is for Dummies.</u>

> *Winners lose more often than losers lose.*
>
> *They learn from the experience.*
>
> *Granma C.*

None of the above is meant to demean my background. On our dairy farm, we ate well. We were taught to eat with our mouth closed and not talk with a full mouth. We didn't burp or lay on the table with our elbows while eating. We didn't hold our fork as though it was a pitchfork or our knife as though we were planning to stab a piece of meat. We were always gracious about thanking the cook for the good nourishing meal we had just enjoyed. But, as Mother used to say, "We don't cook gourmet".

Still there is another world out there and if you want to be taken seriously and compete at an advantage in that environment, for your own sake, ask questions of someone who was trained in etiquette, read books on the subject, watch others who know what to do and then practice at home. No one wants to work with a fellow employee or for a boss of whom they are ashamed. Confidence comes from doing the little things properly, Make good manners a habit.

A restaurant is not the place to teach table manners.

Granma C.

While I'm on the subject of eating, let me share an observation. It seems to me that there are two signs of a good salesperson. 1) they always know the good places to eat and 2) they know how much they have sold so far this month. To prevent you from making many of the mistakes that I have already made, let me pass along some hints for finding good places to eat and avoiding the bad ones.

1. Eat food produced locally (peaches in Georgia, beef in Kansas City, kosher in NYC and seafood on the coast. The only exception to this rule is Boston cream pie in Boston. If there is no local product, order canned vegetable soup and a grilled cheese sandwich.

2. Don't bother to sit down in a restaurant that has dirty tables.

3. Never eat in anything that moves (restaurants on top of buildings, trains, airplanes or your own automobile).

4. Never eat anywhere that is based on All You Can Eat. If you do, use a trough instead of a plate.

5. Never eat in a place called "Mom's" or "Grandma's".

6. Avoid theme restaurants where the servers dress like pirates, cowboys, animals, pixies or elves. Equally bad are restaurants where they cut off your necktie.

Good Personal Hygiene and Appearance are not easy to discuss but since I believe they are both vital to your success, here goes. Your first impression begins even before you walk into the prospect's office. The person you speak with on the telephone may have tremendous influence on the buyer's decision. For every buyer you see, there are eleven unseen buying influences. McGraw Hill publishing company produced this remarkable bit of research data. Their purpose was to emphasize the importance of trade magazines and the ability of other printed matter to penetrate a customer organization more deeply than any salesperson possibly could. Even the receptionist can be a friend and ally. They know more about what is going on in their organization than you could possibly ever know. They are sitting on top of the communications center and they can help guide you.

You only get one chance to make a good first impression.

Granma C.

Some of the things that you can do to make a good first impression are so simple as to almost seem unworthy of mention. Still, I have worked with many salespeople who do not practice these basic skills. Practice them until you do them without having to think about it.

Understand the power of a <u>SMILE</u>. Please try a little experiment. For a day, walk around with the corners of your mouth turned up. If you haven't been accustomed to smiling it may take several days of trying to develop a habit of smiling. When it becomes a habit, you will be surprised at how many people smile back at you. You may even be surprised at how many people ask what you are so happy about. In any case, you make yourself so much more approachable. Put a smile on your face and watch how your mood changes. I knew smiling was a winning habit when customers would say, "Bill, I like for you to call on us because you always come in with a smile". A smile can even be heard over the telephone. It's effortless, but priceless.

It takes 72 muscles to frown, only 14 to smile.

Granma C.

Manner of Dress may vary from call to call or from industry to industry. As a general rule, it is wise to dress similar to the person on whom you are calling. When in doubt, it is better to have dressed up rather than have dressed down. Your dress sends the message that you are a person to be taken seriously.

We are not born knowing how to dress. And it is not a matter of relying on your instincts. There are definite rights and wrongs and if you weren't raised in a family with impeccable taste or you aspire to a higher achievement level than your family, you need qualified guidance. There are sales people at good men's and women's stores who know clothing. Find one of these professionals. Ask for their help in assembling a proper wardrobe. They can help you select clothing within your budget over a period of time. Their knowledge and advice will enable you to dress to your best personal advantage. These individuals take great pride in giving you good guidance. In fact, a good way to identify one of these salespeople is by asking your boss or someone you admire, "whom do you use to help select your wardrobe?" You will be surprised how many successful people have someone upon whom they rely.

Your image is the accumulation

of all the impressions you make.

Granma C.

As a young salesman, I was eligible for the top national award at our annual sales meeting. Knowing that I needed help, my District Manager-Don, asked me what I planned to wear to the ceremony. Naturally, I intended to dress just like I always did. He said, "Bill, you need to start dressing like a businessman. You need to wear long dress hose that cover your hairy legs, a white shirt with a necktie instead of a sport shirt with a bolo tie. And you need a new suit in a conservative color that fits you". Pretty clear, eh?

Don didn't say these things to hurt my feelings. He saw a future for me with the company and he didn't want people from headquarters to write me off as a hick kid. Whether we like it or not, we all wear uniforms or clothing that says a great deal about who we are. The uniform of a businessman is composed of a suit, ironed shirt, tie, dress socks and polished shoes.

If you are shy about revealing your uncertainly in the matter of dress, there are two books that I would recommend. 1) Dress for Success by John T. Molloy and 2) The Power Look by Egon von Furstenberg with Camille Duhe. Developing a good, affordable wardrobe starts with a plan. In this way, you accumulate attractive, appropriate clothing over a period of time. Dressing appropriately doesn't mean that you have to stifle your individuality. You can still use personal touches in the form of accessories, jewelry, kerchief or necktie. There is a Power Look. Dress is a vital part of appearing authoritative and at ease with yourself.

When the student is ready, the teacher appears.

Granma C.

When you look into the eyes of a person, it inspires trust and confidence. Most people do a poor job of <u>eye contact.</u> They look at shoulders, foreheads or other parts of the anatomy. An easy way to check if you are establishing eye contact is to look away and ask yourself, "What color are her eyes"? Looking people in the eye communicates a genuine interest in them and in what you are saying. Also, by doing this, you will pick up cues and improve the quality of your communications with other people.

The human eye is the window to the soul.

Granma C.

Watch effective communicators. They have excellent eye contact. This certainly doesn't mean staring down other people or making them uncomfortable. People from the Middle East and the Pacific Rim are taught as children that lowering their eyes is a sign of decorum. Thus they can be made very uncomfortable by strong eye contact. Be aware of such circumstances, e.g. we worked for several years with Mitsubishi and their Japanese employees. Unlike Americans who tend to become very friendly on short acquaintance, most Orientals have three distinct levels of intimacy.

At first you are a business acquaintance. Given time and good experience with each other, they may choose to consider you as a business friend and enjoy socializing with you at restaurants and night clubs. The status reserved for very few is that of a trusted friend. At this stage, you are invited into their homes to meet their spouse and children. It is important for Americans to realize that this process cannot be rushed. And you are advised to let your Oriental acquaintances take the lead in letting you know at what stage they consider your relationship to be. Any other action is considered rude.

Still, good eye contact emphasizes that what you are saying is important to you. Eyes turned up to the ceiling or down the hall sends the message that you lack self confidence or that there is someone else more important than the one to whom you are talking. Looking people in the eye sends the right message about you and about your attitude toward the person to whom you are talking.

Most buyers are somewhat conservative. Generally older men and women don't favor facial hair. Conversely, men and women in their 30's generally do like facial hair. In fields such as banking, law or sales, if you insist on wearing facial hair, it could have a negative effect on your career. On the other hand in creative fields such as movie/theater, writing and advertising, it may have a positive effect. Being hirsute should be a conscious decision. If you choose to wear hair on your face, keep it groomed. A good rule is to keep hair out of your eyes and off your collar. In the late 1800's only the master of the house wore facial hair. It was a badge of privilege and masculinity. Today, it can be more the expression of a free spirit. Some men feel that it makes them look stronger (a throwback to Samson), more authoritative, more mature, sexier or hipper. If you choose a beard or mustache, be especially careful about eating, drinking or smoking. No one appreciates facial hair that reeks of stale smoke, or glistens with dried dribbles or has crumb garlands. Almost any investment in hair care is a good one. The healthy head of well-cut hair is a major sex and status symbol. Your hairstyle should be coordinated with the clothing style that you have selected.

What can be said of hair can also be said of nails, teeth and skin. A person dealing the public, such as a salesperson, must always be conscious of good grooming. It certainly goes without saying that all of the above should be kept clean and their appearance enhanced by use of conditioners, deodorants, fragrances, lubricants and professional care when appropriate.

If they admire your aftershave or perfume

from across the room, you've used too much.

Granma C.

The comfortable space between two Americans, in a business conversation, is about 2-4 feet. When you notice the person to whom you are speaking take several steps backwards, you may need to pop a mint. Certainly, if someone offers you a mint, don't be offended but readily accept the offer. It is a friendly gesture designed to continue the intercourse. They may be graciously alerting you to the fact that you have buffalo breath. Sales people have enough hurdles to jump without vaporizing the prospective buyer. If you are going to visit clients in the afternoon, it is a considerate practice to not eat Mexican food, onions, garlic or drink alcohol. Of course, if you are with a client who wants to imbibe over lunch, you have a dilemma. Here you may use the piece of advice from the President of U.S. Steel put into a memo to his purchasing department, "If you insist on drinking at lunch, then please don't drink vodka. Drink something that stinks on your breath so that people who come in contact with you will know that you are drunk and not stupid". DON"T make sales calls with booze, tobacco or garlic/onion food on your breath.

Set Personal Goals. As I have worked with and observed people over the years, I have come to the conclusion that it is neither ability nor intelligence that separates achievers from the also-rans.. The difference is that achievers set goals for themselves. They inventory their strengths. Yes, you are surprised that I didn't say strengths AND weaknesses. If you think more about this subject, you will realize, as I finally did, that your strengths and weaknesses are two sides of the same coin. For example, people say to me, "Bill, you really gets things done". They might have also said, "Bill you are demanding and impatient". They are the very same characteristics. It all depends if you want to view them as positive or negative. Knowing this, now, you need to focus on making your strengths work for you. Focusing on eliminating your weaknesses is a lose/lose proposition. The same is true of the people who work with or for you. Identify their strengths and help them put those strengths to work for the organization. This is a win/win proposition. Here is how to get started on setting goals and achieving them.

Write A Personal Mission Statement. This exercise is designed to get you aligned with you; to get to know who you are and what you want out of life. A good way to find out about yourself is put some things down on paper. What is important to you? If you were to die tonight, what would a relative, friend, fellow worker or neighbor have to say about you? Is that what you would want said about you at your funeral? What are you going to do about it? Writing out the answers to the above questions or your own obituary will give you a good start on a personal mission statement. When you have your mission statement in writing, share it with a mentor or good friend. People can help you if they know what you want. It will help you by making your efforts more directional and your energies focused on what is important.

If you don't know where you are going,

any road will get you there.

Granma C.

Macroplan your time. People who are disorganized actually take a great deal of pride in how quickly they can change direction. They typically do what is urgent rather than what is important. If you will set out a 3-week plan, you will find that you do a very good job of listing things that need to be done and in the order of their importance for about 3-4 days. Then, all of a sudden, you will think of something that is really important that needs to be done earlier. Now, you'll have to go back and do some rearranging. By the time you have it stretched out to 3 weeks, you have a framework within which you can really make productive use of your time. You'll be amused at how often other people will accommodate to your schedule because you have a sense of direction. Next, make this 3 week plan into a rolling plan updating it each week for another week. You never run out of a plan.

Microplan your time. Now that your 3-week blueprint for time management is in place, you need to think about what you are going to do on a daily basis. A good habit to develop is at the end of the day, make MUST DO, SHOULD DO, and COULD DO lists for tomorrow. By looking at tomorrow's schedule tonight, you are flying the airplane instead of it flying you. Doing this before you go to bed lets your subconscious mind work out some of the difficulties. Some of my best ideas come to me in bed, not necessarily business related. I also make it a practice to have a notepad and pencil beside my bed. If the idea wakes you, get up and write it down. If you don't, you"ll be searching for it the next morning.

Microplanning involves being prepared for the worst-case scenario. Think about what could go wrong. Take 5 minutes in your car or a convenient Starbucks to make a note of your call objectives. Then do the inventory of the things you may need on the call. For sure, do a quick check of the basics: business cards, pen/pencil, sales tools, calculator, credit cards, and an orderly briefcase (how many times have you suffered for a salesperson who, while bumbling through a handful of disorganized papers, keeps mumbling, "I know it's here somewhere". Have your tools sharp. Have some extra file folders. Label the folders and organize your materials. Be a Pro.

The sign of a true professional

is that they make it look easy.

Granma C.

Eat Your Spinach First. This means that you should do the things you enjoy least, first. Your MUST DO's for the day are those drop-dead things- the things that absolutely have to be done today. Even so, it has been my experience that if I do the distasteful tasks first, I always find time to do the things that I enjoy doing. You will also. It's human nature. Another good habit is to look for recurring problems Instead of fighting the same old dragons every day, trace the recurring problems back to their source. Eliminate the source and you've freed up a big chunk of time. People will marvel at how much you can get done in one day. You may want to promise yourself a reward for completing your list each day.

The future tense of try is triumph.

Granma C.

I learned the <u>recurring problem concept</u> of managing from a young man, John Reidy, who worked with me in Tennessee. When I took over as Director of Marketing, my sales service and field support function was a demoralized outfit that made incredulous mistakes and seemed incapable of getting anything right. They were good, intelligent, motivated people but when you threw them the ball, they dropped it in the middle of the floor. John was fresh out of Harvard B School and it was with some trepidation that I put him in charge of this distressed operation. However, much to my satisfaction, it was not six weeks until I could walk through his department and people were smiling. I began hearing good things back from the field. In other words, the same people who had performed like a cage full of neurotic monkeys were now organized, making customers and field people happy and , more importantly, seemed to be enjoying their jobs. I asked John, "What happened"? "What did you do"? His answer was that he had met with everyone in the department, had them make a list of recurring problems and had them trace the problem back to its origin. Once the source of the problem was identified, it was usually possible to eliminate it. This was one of the dramatic bits of good management at work that I had ever seen. John is now president of the company.

Most big problems should have

been solved while they were small.

Granma C.

Characteristics of well developed goals

1. GOALS ARE IN WRITING. Putting your goals in writing helps to clarify your thinking. It engraves the goal in your mind. Several months later, it can be instructive to see what you put on paper at an earlier date.

2. MAKE GOALS REALISTIC. Goals should cause you to stretch and require more than ordinary hard work. You should challenge yourself. Tell others about your goals. It makes you committed.

3. MAKE YOUR GOALS SPECIFIC AND MEASUREABLE, IF POSSIBLE. Try to describe your goals in dollars, units or %. You can also measure success by setting a deadline or timetable.

4. SET A DEADLINE. A goal is just wishful thinking until you set a deadline. Assigning a time makes you more directional and productive. In fact, setting intermediate deadlines help you achieve a major goal on time. Did you know that there is a national association of procrastinators? Well there is but they haven't held their first meeting yet.

5. VISUALIZE. At night before you go to sleep imagine yourself enjoying the achievement of your goal. Your subconscious mind will go to work for you. The power of the subconscious is just beginning to be understood and appreciated. Using your subconscious is like having your own private genie.

6. BE FLEXIBLE. The only thing in our environment that is certain is CHANGE. Be in charge of change. Regularly re-examine your goals and determine if they are still on target. If not, update them. Of course, don't change weekly or monthly. The magic of goal setting is that it gives you a long term sense of direction.

7. LEARN FROM FAILURE. The trails of successful people are littered with failures. The difference is that they did not use failure as an excuse for quitting. People who succeed fail

more often that failures fail. The achievers learn from their failures. The question is, "Should you go ahead and plow a crooked furrow until you learn how to plow straight"? Or do nothing until you learn how to plow straight? The answer is that you learn to plow by plowing. You learn to perfect your skills while taking action.

WAYS TO INCREASE YOUR PRODUCTIVITY

Learn which customers prefer that you call early or late. One of the best ways to start or end your day is with an order. Almost always, there are major customers who would prefer to see you first thing in the morning or the last thing at night. They know that they are going to buy from you and it enables them to make a better use of their day. One of my favorite memories is about a major buyer in Sandusky, OH. from whom our company had never received an order. Just out of the blue one day, I asked his secretary how to get in to see Mr. Wilson. She laughingly said, "You could meet him for breakfast at Midtown Diner at 6am". Although it required my getting out of bed at 4am and driving 2 hours, I was at the diner the next morning. Sure enough, there he sat at the counter. I sat down beside him and started a conversation. I told him who I was and why I was there. He laughed, paid for my breakfast and gave me an order (about $ 150,000). ***Make your customer's problem your business.*** Don't take a current customer's business for granted. There is always someone out there who is scheming to get your account. Never beout of touch. When you read, hear or just think of an idea that might be of value to your customer, call, clip or write a note and send it to your customer <u>NOW.</u> Ideas are fragile and have a short half-life. Little fill-in reminders from you cause the buyer to think of you first when he/she is buying what you are selling. It could put you first in line. And if you do this well, there may never be a line.

Do you see rocks in your path as barriers

or do you see them as stepping stones?

Granma C.

Make your breaks productive. There are always those times during the day when you cannot make sales calls. Meal time is a big one of those. Imagine how you can extend your productivity when you have breakfast, lunch or dinner with a client. They have to eat also. This does not mean that you always have to be working on a sale but you do get to know each other better and you become top of mind. A word of counsel here. I believe that it is counterproductive to have meals with someone you do not like. As a young salesperson, I thought that I was clever enough to conceal my dislike or distaste for someone. However, as time went by, I picked up from secretaries, assistants and others that their boss really didn't care for me either. Thus, I'm convinced of two things: 1) you aren't going to sell to everybody and 2) people you don't like, usually don't like you either. With people you don't like, I feel it is better to confine your sales call to business hours and get in and get out. Or if you can afford the luxury, don't bother calling on them at all. My experience convinced me that calling on them is <u>not</u> my most productive time.

Do your paperwork NOW. Salespeople are always lamenting that they have too much paperwork. They ask, "Do you want me to make sales or do paperwork"? The answer is, YES i.e. you have to do both. There is a fact that is important. Do you know that the best salespeople are also the best at doing their paperwork. When you think about it, that should not be too surprising. The reason companies want your reports on a timely basis is that it helps them to build a file of market intelligence. This knowledge enables your company to analyze competitive activity on a district or national basis. This intelligence is vital to developing strategies that should give you a competitive advantage. No one does paperwork because it is fun. They do it because it is important.

J&J had a clever way of getting your daily call report. It was one part of a two part form. The other part of the form was your daily expense report. The expense account did not get paid if you didn't do your call reports. I found the best routine was to sit down in the hotel room for about 30 minutes and do the reports before going out to eat. Think about the message you are sending to the home office.

Get and keep the prospect's attention. When you walk into a prospect's office, don't just start talking. Establish that you have their attention. If you don't, you are wasting your bullets. Often they are busy, real or imagined. If they say, "Go ahead, I'm listening" but they are shuffling through papers or looking out the window, just sit quietly. If necessary, say "That's OK. Finish what you are doing because what I have to say is important for you to hear". If you don't feel that way, you shouldn't be there wasting everyone's time. Some little tricks for keeping attention are:

1. <u>Counting your sales points on your fingers</u>. It gives the prospect something to focus on and improves recall.

2. <u>Learn to write upside down.</u> When you are making a calculation to make your point, it is easy for the buyer to follow your reasoning if the numbers are written so it is easy for them to read. Naturally, they will be fascinated with your skill but they will also get your point.

3. <u>Pretend to lose your thought.</u> If you suspect that they are looking but not listening, you can give them a quick cure by stopping and asking, "What was I saying"? Yes, it may make you seem as though you are forgetful but it will serve notice that they better be listening next time.

4. <u>Use your pen.</u> If you are making a point from a piece of sales literature, point to it with your pen. A pointer or something underlined will guide the eye. Not only do you have their attention but you can see and read the point that you are making.

5. "<u>As You Know</u>" is a magic phrase. You may recall having seen it several times in this dissertation. As you know, compliments your listener while at the same time enabling you to make an important point and one that they want to be sure to remember the next time.

6. <u>We are here to work out a way to continue doing business with you.</u> This line is particularly powerful if you have your credit manager with you and your job is to collect money. It overcomes a lot of negatives associated with the situation.

7. <u>This morning I talked to God. What do I have to do to talk with you?</u> Write this on your business card and send it into Mr./Ms. Big. This is a last ditch device for getting in to see someone whom you tried to see on several occasions. Of course, you had better be sure that your mouth is filled with worthwhile stuff. Else you'll be minced meat.

Getting Ready For The Sales Presentation. The sale can be made or lost before you get into the presence of the prospect. The salesperson who doesn't do the needed homework is the one who has to settle for scraps off the table. Get answers to the following questions:

1. What are the prospect's needs and objectives?

2. What are your company's needs and objectives?

3. Is there a situation where $1+1=3$? Is there an incompatibility? Is it easier for you or your prospect to change? Who will benefit most from changing?

4. Gather intelligence (products, economic factors, psychological factors, and competitive strengths).

5. Develop a strategy; a written plan of what you propose to do for what anticipated end result.

6. You need an attention getting opening, e.g. "Are you willing to invest 15 minutes of your time in listening to an idea that will give your company a competitive advantage"? "Would you consider closing this location if I could show you an opportunity available three blocks from here"?

There is nothing better for developing self-confidence than knowing what you are talking about. And there is nothing like knowing what you are talking about to get you a hearing with the decision maker. Speaking about the decision maker, what do you know about him/her? Find out if they are a person who selects their vendors mostly on a personal basis, mostly on a ream of facts and data or do they procrastinate in making decisions. Knowing about personal decision making characteristics can help you be more productive.

There are slick, glib salespeople who can hum a few bars and fake it. I call them "Alligator mouth and hummingbird ass". They talk a good game, promise anything and then deliver only excuses. I can tell you who the winners are in the sales game. They are the individuals who have done their homework and are excited about what they have put together. Now that you are prepared, let's talk about getting in to see Mr./Ms. Big.

The person with the least to say

usually takes the longest to do it.

Granma C.

Almost every busy person has a gatekeeper whose job it is to keep out those people who waste time. So be prepared to qualify yourself. You might be referred by someone they know (be sure this is true). You might have a letter introducing yourself and indicate that you intend to call for an appointment. Write a letter and tell them when you are going to call and then do it (being punctual and businesslike can be the beginning of your credibility with them). You can call on the telephone and tell the gatekeeper what's in it for her boss. You may even be brash enough to ask the gatekeeper, "Who is responsible for innovation and profits"? If you use a brash approach, be prepared to deliver or you'll never get back in.

The secret ingredient in successful

communications is the truth.

Granma C.

Getting the appointment is a vital step. Since getting an appointment can be difficult at times, many salespeople decide to just "drop-in". Drop-ins take a chance that the prospect is not in or not available. They also run the risk of irritating people who are organized and schedule their time. Some thoughts about making appointments are worth considering:

1. It adds to your professional image and enhances the perceived importance of your visit.

2. It assures that you are seeing the right person at his/her convenience.

3. When asking for an appointment always clearly identify yourself and your company. Getting an appointment by subterfuge will ultimately backfire.

4. Get to the point quickly. Have your opening line prepared. It should be designed to stimulate interest. You should hold forth a promise and answer the question, "What's in it for me"?

5. Make your appointment personally. Only you, with your tone of voice, can project the importance of your visit. Use downtime to call for appointments.

6. Never forget that Mr./Ms. Big's assistant can be a very helpful ally. Most people like to be helpful.

> *It is more important to be human*
>
> *than to be important.*
>
> *Granma C.*

Be Prepared. Be Brief. Be Seated.

Too many salespeople think they are good because they are good talkers. Let me tell you something here and now. Good salespeople <u>LISTEN</u> prospects into buying rather than talking them into buying. If you watch a really good salesperson in action, you will see that they have good questions that are designed to find out about the buyer's likes, dislikes, values and needs. A really good real estate agent asks, "What did you like best about your previous home"? A good insurance salesperson asks, "How do you plan to provide for the education of your children in case you are not here to do it"? They ask many good questions and they <u>LISTEN</u> to the answers.

Most people do not mind taking the time to share their innermost thoughts if they perceive that your objective is to help them make a good decision that is in their best interest. Equip yourself with the technical expertise to perform that function on their behalf and you will always be welcome back.

When the prospect welcomes you into their office or home is not the time to "hum a few bars and fake it". You should have come prepared with a list of:

1. Features interpret into benefits. Remember no one wants to buy a 1/4" drill. They want 1/4" holes. You need to know your features but each of them should be converted into a benefit to your prospect. Sell the "sizzle" not the steak. Benefits communicate at the gut level. They motivate buying action. A piece of literature gives a list of features. If that is all your prospect needs, your company doesn't need you.

2. Have your sales tools sharpened. Make sure your brief case contains samples, literature, charts, calculator, a pen and business cards.

3. Have proof statements such as case histories, comparisons demonstrations and testimonials.

4. Write a summary or chart of your closing points.

5. Rehearse. The reason accomplished salespeople make it look so easy is that they have rehearsed. This can be done in the bathroom in the morning, in the car while driving or while taking a stroll. Do you think the top producers just have more talent? Hell No. The top producers do what the bottom producers are unwilling to do. They are prepared.

What are the steps in a sales presentation?

Every book you read will give you different advice and will give you a list of steps from 1 to 10. I have preferred to use a simple 4-step device to help organize my sales presentation.

It is called AIDA.

Attention - Have a dramatic opening that cannot be ignored e.g "This came off one of your products" or "Who do you think used this last"?

Interest - Show and Tell. Demonstrate. Get the buyer involved. If you get them physically involved, they will be mentally involved. A good sales person is a teacher, an actor and a storyteller. Cultivate your skills by working with children. They'll let you know when you are good at it.

Desire - What's in it for her/him? Use analogies, metaphors. Emphasize benefit. Get them imagining how they would feel or be appreciated for investing in your offering. Most people do not buy for logical reasons. They use their intellect to convince themselves that they are doing the right thing. Buyers want acceptance, wealth, health, appetites gratified, to be amused, have security and to look great. It is your job to show them how they can achieve these desires by making a Decision, right now.

Action - Most people will use all types of devices to avoid or postpone making a decision. This is where your self-confidence is reassuring to them. The ability to get people to trust you is important and it has to be earned. Trust comes from all that you have done and said today and in the past. If the decision is in the buyer's best interest and they don't make the decision today, you have cut the chance of ever getting the order in half. And have multiplied the chance that another sales person will get the order soon.

Lord, fill my mouth with worthwhile stuff

and sit me down when I've said enough.

Granma C.

Let Your Personality Show Through.

Everyone is not going to think that you are the greatest thing since sliced bread. The important thing is to learn what works best for you. If you try to pattern your sales style after another sales person whom you admire, you will fail. I learned this lesson well from my first District Sales Manager-DuPont Murphy. Duke was a southern colonel and when he made a sales call on a physician, they would have a chatty, amiable visit and when our Coca-Colas, offered by the doctor, were finished, somehow we would walk out with the order and never appeared to talk business. I, being a 22 year old ambitious Yankee , watched him carefully. Because I wanted to be as good as Duke, I tried to pattern myself after his words, gestures and dress. Well, I wouldn't be offered a Coke and I would walk out of a sales call wet-to-my-waist from perspiration and I didn't get an order. Finally, when I confessed my failures to Duke, he told me, "Bill, you have to develop your own style". When I quit trying to be someone else, I began making sales. I'm grateful that I learned that lesson early because it carries over into one's personal life as well.

I can't give you a formula for success

but I can give you a formula for failure,

try to please everybody.

Granma C.

Before I leave, I will give you a creed that I found early in my career and have embellished upon it since that time. It is called the Creed Of A Good Salesperson. Above all, as you consider a career as a salesperson, you need to be able to say, "I am proud to be a salesperson". I believe if you carry this Creed with you or put it somewhere that it can be a constant reminder and attempt to practice its tenets, you will not only be a successful salesperson but you will be a successful human being as well.

Whether we like it or not, every single one of us is involved with the need to sell our ideas. Or, if you prefer, the need to develop persuasive skills to assist in communicating with your significant other, your children, your fellow workers and certainly with your boss.

You had better learn how to communicate

persuasively with other people because there are

so many of them and only one of you.

Granma C.

CREED OF A GOOD SALESPERSON

To be aware of my responsibilities. This includes my responsibility to myself, my family, my company and my customers.

To constantly improve my skills as a communicator. I will scrutinize every part of my selling effort. I will read books, take self-improvement courses and share ideas with other salespeople. I will be a lifelong learner.

To seek a clear understanding of my customer's needs. Your customer values your problem solving ideas. This is how you earn their business.

To place a high value on my time. Plan your work. Work your plan. Others will quickly learn that you do not like for your time to be wasted. This doesn't mean that you don't have time to be friendly and considerate. It just means that you don't waste their time and you appreciate the same consideration.

To know my products and services. Be accurate when you give data and information. Be imaginative in the application of your offering to help others solve problems or build their businesses. Seek new and improved ways that your products/services can deliver more value to your customers.

To be a good listener. Try to determine if you are a good listener. Most people are not. Learn to listen for meaning. Don't worry about what you are going to say next. LISTEN to what they are saying. Watch gestures, selection of words and posture for cues to the importance of what is being said and Activate your radar. Pick up need signals.

To make one more sales call each day. After you have completed the number of calls expected of you, make one more. Job security comes from being worth more than you are paid. Assess each day's work to identify ineffective or faulty work habits that should be eliminated.

To remember the difference between aggressive and assertive.
Aggressiveness produces negative reactions. Assertiveness produces positive reactions. It is the simple difference between being irritating and assuring.

To advance the standards of professional salesmanship. A good salesperson can be proud of his/her contribution to the economic growth of their company and of our country. When in doubt, do what's right.

www.ingramcontent.com/pod-product-compliance
Lightning Source LLC
Chambersburg PA
CBHW051257170526
45165CB00004B/1756